Ocean Party

by Kathy Groth
Illustrated by Briar-Rose Johnson

First Edition: June 2024

5 4 3 2
ISBN-979-8-9887488-1-6
Library of Congress Control Number: 2024911375
Groth, Kathy 1959-

OCEAN PARTY
Ecology-Ocean
Friendship-Relationships
Pollution-plastic

Editor: Kathy Groth
Book Design: Chuck Groth, cover & interior
Illustrator: Briar-Rose Johnson
Gift photography: Tyra Raasch

Loon Calling Press

Loon Calling Press-Kat's Books LLC
PO Box 253
New Richmond, WI 54017
 www.kathygroth.com
715-699-0897

All internal images used with permission by individuals/organizations noted (and with our sincere thanks).

This book is dedicated to all
the young, and
young at heart, ecologists.

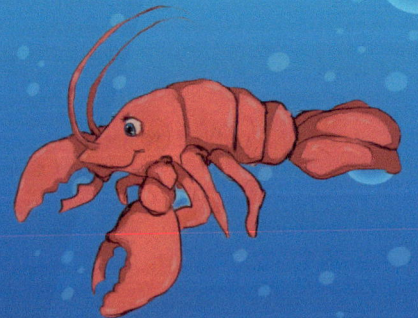

It's Old Turtle's birthday and he's wide awake.

His friends are all ready with gifts they will take.

But poor Clara Clownfish

Doesn't know what she should make.

HI! I'm Patrick Puffer.
What do YOU think Clara
should make?

"Suzy Shark, what did you bring?"

"I made a ring so he'll feel like a king."

Can you guess what she used to make the ring?

"Matteo Manatee, what have you got?

"I made some flowers to put in a pot."

Can you guess what he used to
make the flowers for the pot?

"Wally Whale, what did you bring down?"

"I have been busy making a crown."

Can you guess what he used to make the crown?

"Ophelia Octopus, what is your gift?"

"I made a statue that is heavy to lift."

OLD TURTLE

Can you guess what she used to make the statue?

"Sebastian Seahorse, you made a cake!"

"No, I can't bake so it is a fake."

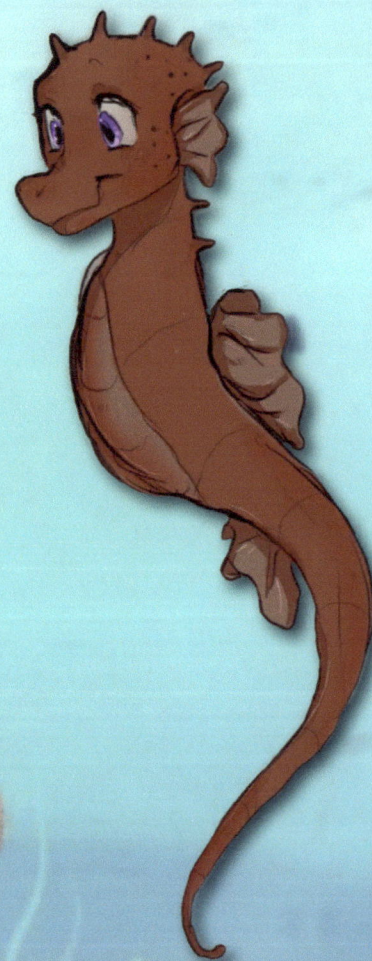

Can you guess what he used to
make the fake cake?

"Jamaal Jellyfish, did you make a cape?

"Yes, around his shoulders it will drape."

Can you guess what he used to make the cape?

"Oh my, Sally Seal, that is beautiful art!"

"I spent a whole day just collecting each part!"

Can you guess what she used to make the picture?

Suddenly something floated down from above!

"This is it! I'll make something Old Turtle will love!"

Can you guess what floated down from above?

Clara Clownfish has come up with a plan,
And off she goes as fast as she can.

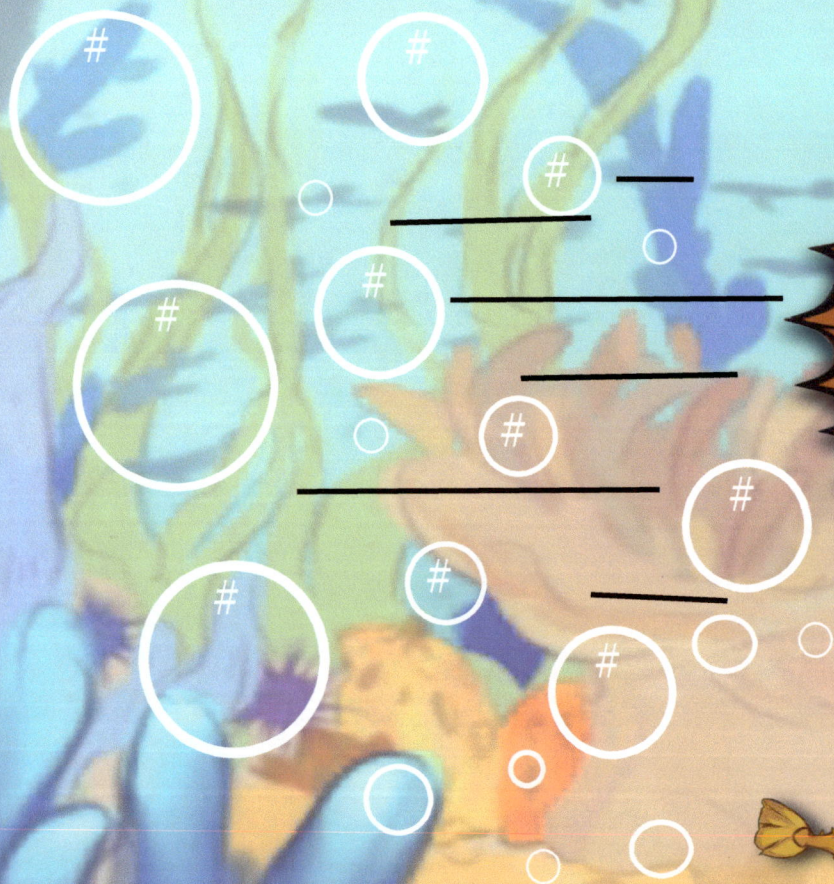

Hey! Wait for me!!

Clara made a necklace of the thing she just found.

She stretched out a hole to make it more round.

"S-T-R-R-E-T-T-C-C-H

Then she added some color onto each loop,

And wrapped it up fast to get back to the group.

Can you guess what she added
to each loop?

Old Turtle saw it and exclaimed with delight,

"This is the perfect gift to end this fun night!"

Latrelle Lobster's pincher worked like a knife,
and her quick action saved Old Turtle's life.

SNAP

PHEW!

Old Turtle says, "This is what I fear."

"These gifts are kind but they don't belong here."

Old Turtle decides to do something drastic.

"We need to get rid of all of this plastic!"

So everyone quickly gathers the trash...

...and goes on enjoying

the birthday bash!

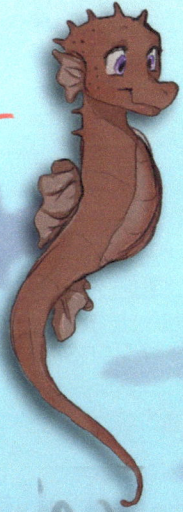

What were the gifts made from?

Crown-plastic straws (cut up and whole) on liter plastic bottle

Ring-plastic bottle cap ring, bottle bottoms

Turtle statue- plastic bags in chicken wire frame with bottle cap eyes

Flowers-plastic bottle bottoms on straws with twist caps wrapped in plastic bags

With sincere thanks, these items were created by the Diedrich, Dubois, Deters families

Cape-plastic laundry jug, bags, bottle caps

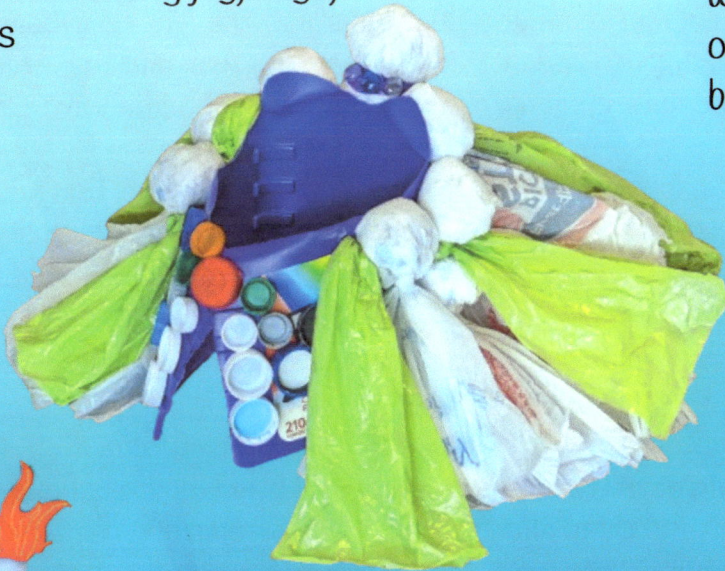

Picture-plastic spoons with bags and bottle caps on frame made of plastic bags on cardboard

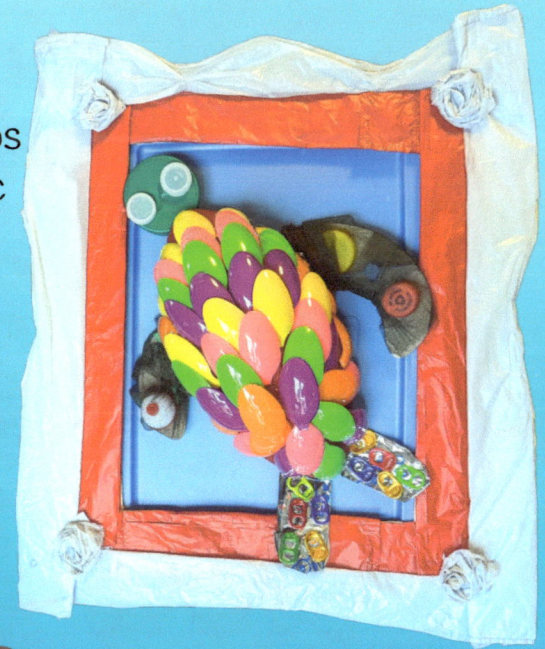

Cake-plastic coffee can, take-out container, cup, straw, bottle caps, topped with toy made to look like a flame (sea ferns and shell added for decoration)

Necklace-Six pack beverage can ring, plastic bottle caps, twist caps, water bottle caps

With sincere thanks, these items were created by the Andracek, Gibson, Raasch, and Shea families

A letter from Old Turtle to all young ecologists,

There is one world ocean that consists of the Pacific Ocean, the Atlantic Ocean, the Indian Ocean, the Southern Ocean, and the Arctic Ocean. Without oceans, humans, animals, and plants couldn't live.

There are billions of pounds of plastic in our oceans. It is killing fish, birds, and sea creatures. Plastic bags floating in the ocean look like jellyfish, which is my main diet. You might not know it, but we can choke on a plastic cap, a straw, or even some fishing line. It's dangerous for your health, too, because fish eat the tiny pieces of plastic and then humans eat the fish.

How can you help? There's a lot that you humans can do to keep trash from ending up in the world's ocean and other bodies of water. Look around you and think about all the plastic items you use every day. Plastic is everywhere. Wrappers, beverage bottles, bottle caps, grocery bags, straws, take-out containers, and even fishing nets. Many plastic products are single-use items that are designed to be thrown away. If this waste isn't properly managed, it can end up in the ocean.

- Try to reduce your use of disposable and single-use plastic items.
- Reuse and/or recycle plastic items.
- You could also help out at a cleanup program, volunteering your time to pick up litter in your local community and waterways near you.

All of us sea creatures would appreciate it if you would leave only your footprints behind when you visit the beach.

Respectfully, Old Turtle

OUR WORLD OCEAN
provides

CLIMATE REGULATION

70% Covering 70% of the Earth's surface, the ocean transports heat from the equator to the poles, regulating our climate and weather patterns.

ECONOMY

$282 billion Amount the U.S. ocean economy produces in goods and services. Ocean-dependent businesses employ almost 3 million people.

TRANSPORTATION

76% Percent of all U.S. trade involving some form of marine transportation.

RECREATION

From fishing to boating to kayaking and whale watching, the ocean provides us with so many unique activities.

FOOD

The ocean provides much more than just seafood. Ingredients from the sea are found in surprising foods such as peanut butter and soymilk.

MEDICINE

Many medicinal products come from the ocean, including ingredients that help fight cancer, arthritis, Alzheimer's disease, and heart disease.

Graphic courtesy of National Oceanic and Atmospheric Administration (NOAA)

Thanks to the water cycle, oceans give us rainwater and drinking water.

The oceans cover nearly 71% of Earth's surface. They contain about 97% of all the water on Earth.

Plastic waste makes up about 80% of all ocean pollution. Once in the water, plastic doesn't totally decompose, so as it's being tossed around, much of it breaks down into tiny pieces called microplastics.

At least half of the air we breathe comes from plants in the ocean. Ocean plants take in carbon dioxide and give us oxygen.

Let's talk...

—If you were one of the sea creatures in this story, how would YOU get rid of the plastic trash they had collected?

—What can WE do to keep our world ocean and beaches clean?

—What can YOU do to keep OUR Earth clean and green?

Draw a picture of YOU helping to clean up YOUR neighborhood.

OCEAN PARTY
LANGUAGE ARTS LESSON PLAN

After reading the story, <u>Ocean Party</u>, students will act it out with the puppets, using dialogue from the story to better understand the text.

Objectives
    –Students will listen to the read-aloud and understand the text.
    –Students will be able to retell the story in sequence through a puppet play.
    –Students will improve fluency through repeated readings until their puppet play part is memorized.
    –Students will be able to speak clearly at an understandable volume and pace.

Standards
    CCSS.ELA-L.2.1
    CCSS.ELA-L.2.3
    CCSS.SL.2.2
    CCSS.SL.2.4

Materials
    –Sea creature cut-outs
    –Tongue depressors or popsicle sticks
    –Hot glue gun, glue, or stapler
    –Book: <u>Ocean Party</u>

Procedure

—Activate prior knowledge about oceans and sea creatures. Introduce the title and discuss it.

—Read aloud <u>Ocean Party</u>, stopping to introduce each character and check for understanding.

—Divide students into groups of twelve (eleven sea creatures and a narrator).

—Cut out the sea creature shapes on the following pages for puppets, or make copies of them to cut out.

—Glue the sea creature puppets onto small paper plates.

—Attach a tongue depressor or popsicle stick to the back of each paper plate.

—Practice retelling the story in sequence, using the book for younger students (the teacher reads voice parts as the students repeat them until memorized) or for students who can read (individual scripts copied from the book with repeated readings until memorized). The narrator can be the teacher or a more advanced reader.

—Perform as a puppet play(s).

—Discuss after the puppet play(s) what the students have learned about the book and introduce them to the word ECOLOGY (the relationship between humans and their physical environment).

—Share what each of us can do to keep our oceans and other waterways clean.

About the Author

Kathy (Ackley) Groth lives with her husband Chuck, in Northern Wisconsin half the year and Florida the other half. Kathy taught elementary school for many years. She and Chuck raised two daughters and enjoy the company of five grandchildren. Now retired, Kathy shares her passion for education through children's literature, inspiring curiosity and wonder in children through her second career as an author. Her love for children and children's literature has always been her inspiration.

For more information about Kathy's books and teachers' guides, visit her website at www.kathygroth.com.

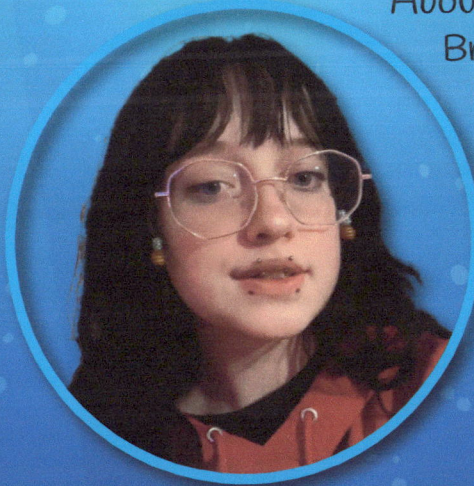

About the Illustrator

Briar-Rose Johnson and Kathy met at their local book club in 2023. They hit it off right away and Kathy was pleasantly surprised to find out Briar has a talent for drawing, especially sea creatures.

Briar is 20 years old and lives in Roberts, Wisconsin. She plans to go to college for digital art. She hopes to illustrate her own books someday, create graphic novels, and design video games. Since childhood, Briar has always had a great imagination and felt drawing was fun, which fed her creative spirit.

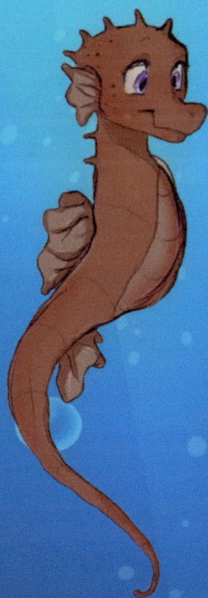

www.ingramcontent.com/pod-product-compliance
Lightning Source LLC
Chambersburg PA
CBHW041552030426

42335CB00005B/190